WOLVES
POSTCARDS

COLLECTION TWO

◁ **W9-CNN-999**

Twenty-two postcards
to benefit the
**INTERNATIONAL
WOLF CENTER**

Voyageur Press

Introduction and captions by Todd R. Berger
Printed in Hong Kong
94 95 96 97 98 5 4 3 2 1

ISBN 0-89658-256-6

Distributed in Canada by Raincoast Books, 112 East Third Avenue, Vancouver, B.C. V5T 1C8

Published by Voyageur Press, Inc.
P.O. Box 338, 123 North Second Street, Stillwater, MN 55082 U.S.A.
612-430-2210, *fax* 612-430-2211

Please write or call, or stop by, for our free catalog of natural history publications. Our toll-free number to place an order or to obtain a free catalog is 800-888-WOLF (800-888-9653).

Educators, fundraisers, premium and gift buyers, publicists, and marketing managers: Looking for creative products and new sales ideas? Voyageur Press books are available at special discounts when purchased in quantities, and special editions can be created to your specifications. For details contact the marketing department.

The International Wolf Center

At the International Wolf Center, visitors experience the stirring howl of the wolf in the combined setting of museum and nature center. The center is located in Ely, Minnesota, in the heart of wolf range and the site of twenty-five years of wolf research. The center's mission of public education about the wolf and its interrelationships with other species is its driving force. There, visitors learn about the wolf's story, its habits, and its coexistence with other species and with humans. Contact the International Wolf Center for more information about membership, or join now at one of of the following levels and receive *International Wolf*, the quarterly educational magazine for IWC members.

☐ $25 Lone Wolf
☐ $50 Wolf Pack
☐ $100 Wolf Associate
☐ $500 Wolf Sponsor
☐ $1000 Alpha Wolf

International Wolf Center
1396 Highway 169
Ely, Minnesota 55731-8129 U.S.A.
1-800-ELY-WOLF (1-800-359-9653)

Cover: Photograph copyright © and donated by Bruce Montagne
Page 1: Staring is a common way for alpha wolves to assert dominance over the other members of the pack. The subordinate wolves know their place after seeing the glare of their leader. *(Photograph copyright © and donated by Rick McIntyre)*

The noble wolf once ranged across North America, as far south as what was to become Mexico City. In fact, the wolf was one of the most wide-ranging animals in the world.

Native Americans of almost every tribe across the continent knew of the wolf, which shared their land. They honored and respected the wolf, seeing great similarity between the wolf's hunting behavior and pack society and their own society. They believed the wolf had a soul.

The European settlers saw the wolf from a different point of view. The settlers had a long history of attempts to eradicate wolves. They believed the carnivorous wolf not only didn't have a soul, but had a heart of stone. Wolves were considered a danger to their cattle, their wild prey, and themselves.

As the New World grew in population, and large areas of wilderness were developed, the wolf was either killed or pushed back out of the settled areas. Even organizations such as the National Park Service were involved in killing wolves. The wolves were exterminated in their traditional range, and today, though they survive in large numbers in Canada and Alaska, wolves have only a small foothold in the contiguous United States, the largest population living in northern Minnesota.

Northern Minnesota is also the home of the International Wolf Center, which is dedicated to educating the world about the endangered wolf. In addition, wolf reintroduction programs at places like Yellowstone National Park, Great Smoky Mountains National Park, and North Carolina's Alligator River National Wildlife Refuge are trying to bring the wolf back into its natural range. The survival of the beautiful wolf has become a priority for many, and should be a priority for us all.

About the Photographers

The wolf photographers for *Wolves Postcards, Collection Two*, are Rick McIntyre, wildlife photographer and author of *A Society of Wolves: National Parks and the Battle Over the Wolf*; Lynn Rogers of St. Paul, Minnesota, author, photographer, and former wildlife research biologist for the U.S. Forest Service; L. David Mech of St. Paul, Minnesota, wildlife research biologist for the U.S. National Biological Survey, and author/photographer of several books about wolves; Karen Hollett of Mount St. Vincent University, Halifax, Nova Scotia; Monty Sloan, wildlife photographer, from Wolf Park, Battle Ground, Indiana; and Bruce Montagne, wildlife photographer, from Milford, Michigan.

These photographers have generously donated some of their best artwork so that all royalties from the sale of the *Wolves Postcards, Collection Two*, will be donated to the International Wolf Center in Ely, Minnesota.

A mating pair of gray wolves walks across a snowy scene. Winter can be harsh in most of the wolves' habitat, but the cold weather and deep snowfalls actually make it easier for wolves to catch their prey who have been weakened by the severe conditions and scarce food.

One of the reasons a wolf howls is to warn potential intruders to keep out of its territory. Wolves will howl in response to the howls of foreign wolves. The International Wolf Center in Ely, Minnesota, takes visitors out on special wolf-howling trips, and the less-inhibited members of these excursions often get a response to their bellows.

Photograph copyright © 1994 and donated by Rick McIntyre. From Wolves Postcards, Collection Two *by the International Wolf Center* 1-800-359-9653. *Published by Voyageur Press* 1-800-888-9653.

A five-week-old wolf pup flashes its baby blues. At this age, the youngster is just starting to explore the outside world, but it still spends a lot of time resting or sleeping.

Photograph copyright © 1994 and donated by Rick McIntyre. From Wolves Postcards, Collection Two *by the International Wolf Center* 1-800-359-9653. *Published by Voyageur Press* 1-800-888-9653.

Noted wolf biologist L. David Mech became an accepted part of this arctic wolf family living in Canada's High Arctic. He was able to get his camera in very close as a mother walked along the barren ground of the High Arctic with two four-week-old pups.

Photograph copyright © 1994 and donated by L. David Mech. From Wolves Postcards, Collection Two *by the International Wolf Center* *1-800-359-9653. Published by Voyageur Press 1-800-888-9653.*

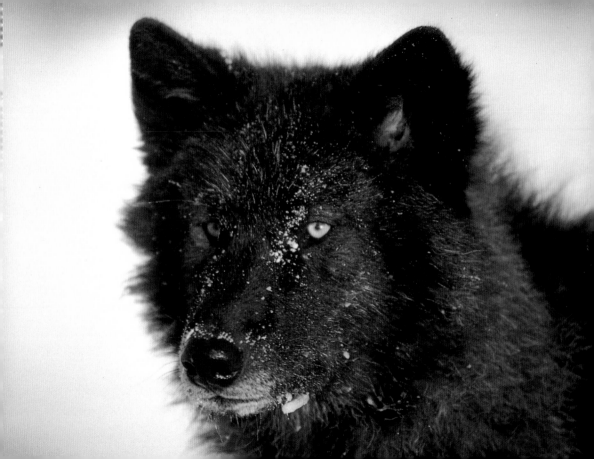

Most wolves are gray. But in southern Canada and most of Alaska, wolves with inky black fur are common.

Photograph copyright © 1994 and donated by Monty Sloan/Wolf Park. From Wolves Postcards, Collection Two *by the International Wolf Center 1-800-359-9653. Published by Voyageur Press 1-800-888-9653.*

A majestic black-colored, or black phase, wolf peers through the autumn leaves in the northern United States. Wolves survive in corners of the United States despite longtime human animosity toward the animals.

Photograph copyright © 1994 and donated by Bruce Montagne. From Wolves Postcards, Collection Two *by the International Wolf Center 1-800-359-9653. Published by Voyageur Press 1-800-888-9653.*

Food is scarce in the High Arctic, and wolf packs often will split up to be able to cover larger areas hunting for food. This solitary arctic wolf travels over the bleak landscape looking for prey to satiate the pack's hunger.

Photograph copyright © 1994 and donated by L. David Mech. From Wolves Postcards, Collection Two *by the International Wolf Center* 1-800-359-9653. *Published by Voyageur Press* 1-800-888-9653.

These playful wolf pups wrestling in the grass are not only exercising their young muscles, they are also practicing behaviors that will be useful when, as adults, they need to defend themselves or go hunting for prey.

Photograph copyright © 1994 and donated by L. David Mech. From Wolves Postcards, Collection Two *by the International Wolf Center* 1-800-359-9653. *Published by Voyageur Press* 1-800-888-9653.

The intelligence of wolves is well documented. Wolves have proven much more adept than dogs at learning through observation and solving problems.

Photograph copyright © 1994 and donated by Bruce Montagne. From Wolves Postcards, Collection Two *by the International Wolf Center* 1-800-359-9653. *Published by Voyageur Press* 1-800-888-9653.

Black wolf packs are most common north of the Canadian border to the Arctic Circle, but occasionally black and gray wolves appear in the same pack in more southerly locales. The genetic reasons for the different shades are, at present, unknown.

Photograph copyright © 1994 and donated by Lynn Rogers. From Wolves Postcards, Collection Two *by the International Wolf Center* *1-800-359-9653. Published by Voyageur Press 1-800-888-9653.*

Wolves originally ranged across almost all of North America. But Europeans brought many customs across the seas, including a hatred of wolves. Though a large population of wolves still inhabits Canada and Alaska, only small pockets of these animals survive in the northern United States, like this gray wolf in Michigan's Upper Peninsula, where about fifty wolves live.

Photograph copyright © 1994 and donated by Bruce Montagne. From Wolves Postcards, Collection Two *by the International Wolf Center 1-800-359-9653. Published by Voyageur Press 1-800-888-9653.*

An arctic wolf pup appears serene as the photographer comes in close for a candid shot. Unlike their cousins to the south, wolves of the High Arctic have evolved without the threat of humans and, therefore, tend not to react in fear to encroaching people.

Photograph copyright © 1994 and donated by L. David Mech. From Wolves Postcards, Collection Two by the International Wolf Center 1-800-359-9653. Published by Voyageur Press 1-800-888-9653.

This beautiful gray wolf may look like a German shepherd or malamute and for good reason. The wolf and dog share many traits, but, unlike its domesticated cousin, the wolf retains its wild characteristics.

Photograph copyright © 1994 and donated by Karen Hollett. From Wolves Postcards, Collection Two by the International Wolf Center 1-800-359-9653. Published by Voyageur Press 1-800-888-9653.

The wolf's speed would be an Olympic track coach's dream come true—that is if wolves were allowed to compete. Wolves can speed along at more than thirty-five miles per hour and can maintain a running gait over great distances.

An adult wolf with black coloring lies on the ground next to a red oak sapling. Despite stereotypes and folktales, a case of a healthy wolf killing a human being in North America has never been documented.

Photograph copyright © 1994 and donated by Bruce Montagne. From Wolves Postcards, Collection Two *by the International Wolf Center* 1-800-359-9653. Published by Voyageur Press 1-800-888-9653.

An arctic wolf hunches its back and looks right down the lens of the camera. The barren landscape and the arctic wolves' relatively little fear of humans makes this photographer a curious oddity to wolves.

Photograph copyright © 1994 and donated by L. David Mech. From Wolves Postcards, Collection Two *by the International Wolf Center* 1-800-359-9653. *Published by Voyageur Press* 1-800-888-9653.

The dominant wolves in a pack are called the alpha male and alpha female. The alpha male eats the choicest parts of captured prey and, having bred with the alpha female, is often the father of the other pack members.

Photograph copyright © 1994 and donated by Rick McIntyre. From Wolves Postcards, Collection Two *by the International Wolf Center* 1-800-359-9653. *Published by Voyageur Press* 1-800-888-9653.

The gray wolf is called by different names in different geographic locations. For example, the arctic wolf is the same species as the timber wolf (*Canis lupus*). This differing nomenclature has, in part, caused disagreement over how many subspecies of wolves there are.

A majestic alpha, or dominant, wolf listens intently to the sounds of the forest. The bold stance and dominant social interaction with other wolves distinguish the alpha male from the more submissive members of the pack.

A magnificent arctic wolf peeks its head over a grassy hill in the High Arctic region of Canada. Wolves, once one of the most widely distributed animals in the world, survive in only remote wilderness areas.

Photograph copyright © 1994 and donated by L. David Mech. From Wolves Postcards, Collection Two by the International Wolf Center 1-800-359-9653. Published by Voyageur Press 1-800-888-9653.

A gray wolf surveys a snowy landscape. Wolves once lived in many areas of the United States, including a large number in Yellowstone National Park. But eradication programs eliminated the wolf from its traditional habitats. No confirmed sightings of resident wolves had occurred near Yellowstone since the 1920s until fall of 1992, when a wolf was killed outside the southeastern border of the park.

Photograph copyright © 1994 and donated by Monty Sloan/Wolf Park. From Wolves Postcards, Collection Two *by the International Wolf Center 1-800-359-9653. Published by Voyageur Press 1-800-888-9653.*

Mom is still close by for these young wolf pups. Though their curiosity about the world grows stronger with each new day, these four-week-old pups won't start to stray too far from their mother until they get a little older.

Photograph copyright © 1994 and donated by L. David Mech. From Wolves Postcards, Collection Two by the International Wolf Center 1-800-359-9653. Published by Voyageur Press 1-800-888-9653.